D0710594

Oachs, Emily Rose,
Africa /
2016.
33305235964313
sa   09/07/16

DISCOVER THE CONTINENTS

Africa

by Emily Rose Oachs

BLASTOFF! READERS

3

BELLWETHER MEDIA · MINNEAPOLIS, MN

Note to Librarians, Teachers, and Parents:

Blastoff! Readers are carefully developed by literacy experts and combine standards-based content with developmentally appropriate text.

Level 1 provides the most support through repetition of high-frequency words, light text, predictable sentence patterns, and strong visual support.

Level 2 offers early readers a bit more challenge through varied simple sentences, increased text load, and less repetition of high-frequency words.

Level 3 advances early-fluent readers toward fluency through increased text and concept load, less reliance on visuals, longer sentences, and more literary language.

Level 4 builds reading stamina by providing more text per page, increased use of punctuation, greater variation in sentence patterns, and increasingly challenging vocabulary.

Level 5 encourages children to move from "learning to read" to "reading to learn" by providing even more text, varied writing styles, and less familiar topics.

Whichever book is right for your reader, Blastoff! Readers are the perfect books to build confidence and encourage a love of reading that will last a lifetime!

This edition first published in 2016 by Bellwether Media, Inc.

No part of this publication may be reproduced in whole or in part without written permission of the publisher. For information regarding permission, write to Bellwether Media, Inc., Attention: Permissions Department, 5357 Penn Avenue South, Minneapolis, MN 55419.

Library of Congress Cataloging-in-Publication Data

Oachs, Emily Rose.
  Africa / by Emily Rose Oachs.
    pages cm. – (Blastoff! Readers: Discover the Continents)
  Includes bibliographical references and index.
  Summary: "Simple text and full-color photography introduce beginning readers to Africa. Developed by literacy experts for students in kindergarten through third grade"– Provided by publisher.
  Audience: Grades K-3.
  ISBN 978-1-62617-323-1 (hardcover : alk. paper)
  1. Africa–Juvenile literature. I. Title.
  DT22.O225 2016
  916–dc23
                            2015028721

Text copyright © 2016 by Bellwether Media, Inc. BLASTOFF! READERS and associated logos are trademarks and/or registered trademarks of Bellwether Media, Inc. SCHOLASTIC, CHILDREN'S PRESS, and associated logos are trademarks and/or registered trademarks of Scholastic Inc.

Printed in the United States of America, North Mankato, MN.

Table of
Contents

Home of Early Humans

Egyptian pyramids

Humans have lived in Africa for thousands of years. Scientists have found bones about 200,000 years old on the **continent**!

DID YOU KNOW?

- Africa has the world's largest hot desert. The Sahara is about the same size as the United States!

- Africa's Nile is the world's longest river.

- As many as 2,000 languages are spoken in Africa!

- Africa is the only continent where giraffes, hippos, ostriches, and lemurs live in the wild.

Nile River

Today, people visit the **ancient** pyramids in Egypt. Victoria Falls is another famous **landmark**. This beautiful waterfall flows in Zambia and Zimbabwe.

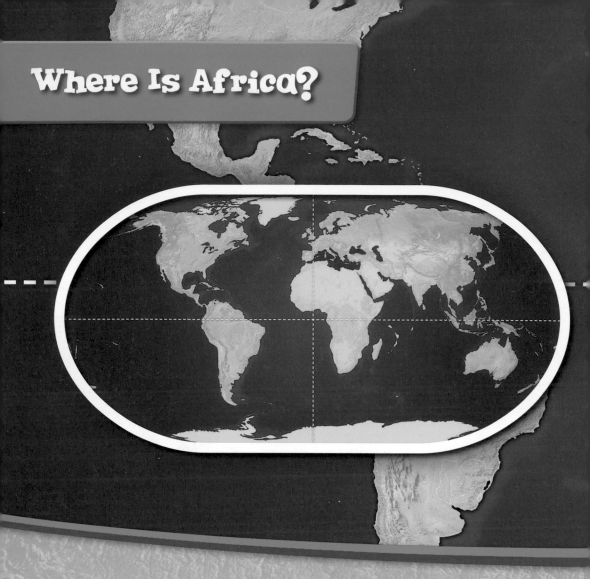

Where Is Africa?

The Mediterranean Sea and
Asia border northern Africa.
Eastern Africa touches the Indian
Ocean. The Atlantic Ocean lies
to the west.

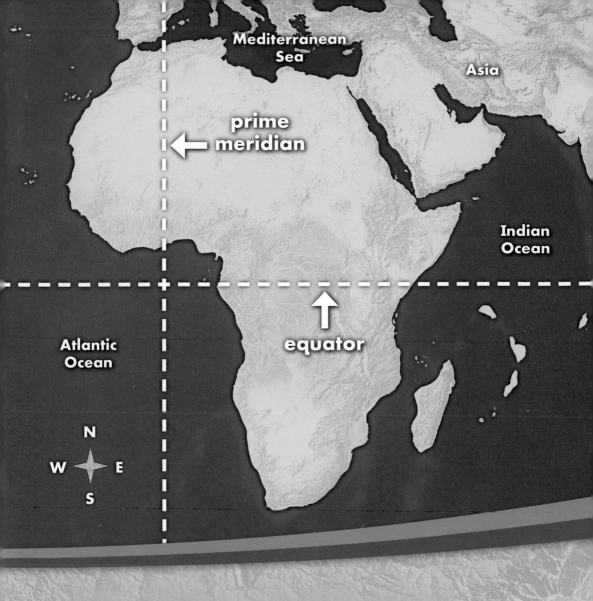

Mediterranean Sea

Asia

prime meridian

Indian Ocean

Atlantic Ocean

equator

N
W E
S

The **prime meridian** and the **equator** cross Africa. This puts the continent in all four **hemispheres**.

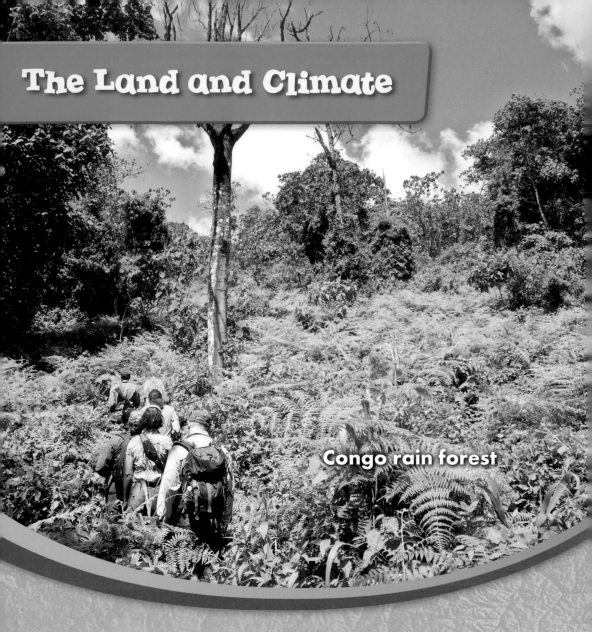

Congo rain forest

Africa's lands are often hot year-round. One **area** is the steamy Congo **rain forest**. It lies near the equator.

The Sahara Desert stretches across northern Africa. The Kalahari and Namib deserts are in southern Africa.

Sahara
Desert

Congo
rain forest

Namib
Desert

Kalahari
Desert

Sahara
Desert

N
W   E
S

Africa has large **savannahs**. These grasslands have rainy seasons and dry seasons. The most famous example is the Serengeti in eastern Africa.

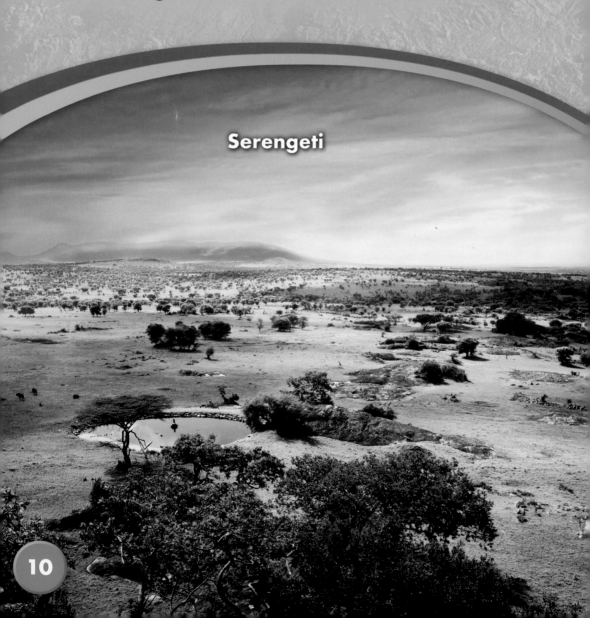

Serengeti

Lake Victoria

Serengeti

N
W E
S

Lake
Victoria

The shores of Lake
Victoria sit west of
the Serengeti. This is
Africa's largest lake.

The Plants and Animals

rain forest

orchids

Orchids bloom in the rain forest. There, vines stretch between okoumé trees.

Tall grasses grow on the savannahs. Hibiscus flowers blossom there. **Shrubs** and acacia trees dot the landscape. Few plants grow in Africa's deserts.

hibiscus flower

acacia trees

Gorillas and chimpanzees play in Africa's rain forests. Scorpions dart across desert sands. On the savannahs, lions and cheetahs hunt zebras.

chimpanzee

scorpion

zebra

lion

wildebeests

Millions of wildebeests live on the Serengeti. Every year, they **migrate** in search of food and water.

The People

Many people call Africa home. More than 1 billion people live there. Only the continent of Asia has a larger **population**.

Tunisia

Morocco

Algeria

Libya

Egypt

Eritrea

Djibouti

Somalia

Senegal

The Gambia

Mauritania

Mali

Niger

Chad

Sudan

Cape Verde

Burkina Faso

Nigeria

Central African Republic

South Sudan

Ethiopia

Ivory Coast

Benin

Cameroon

Seychelles

Liberia

Ghana

Sierra Leone

Togo

Gabon

Uganda

Kenya

Guinea

Guinea-Bissau

Equatorial Guinea

Democratic Republic of the Congo

Rwanda

Burundi

Tanzania

Comoros

Mauritius

São Tomé and Principe

Republic of the Congo

Angola

Zambia

Zimbabwe

Madagascar

Malawi

N
W — E
S

Namibia

Botswana

Mozambique

Swaziland

South Africa

Lesotho

There are 54 countries in Africa. Some of these are islands.

Lagos, Nigeria, is Africa's largest city. More than 21 million people live there. It is one of the world's fastest-growing cities.

Many Africans are moving from the countryside into cities like Lagos. It is a sign of a growing and changing continent.

Fast Facts About Africa

Size: 11,700,000 square miles
(30,300,000 square kilometers);
2nd largest continent

Number of Countries: 54

Largest Country: Algeria

Smallest Country: Seychelles

Number of People: 1.2 billion

Place with Most People: Lagos, Nigeria

Top Natural Resources: diamonds, gold,
wood, fish, natural gas, copper

Top Landmarks:
o Pyramids at Giza (Egypt)
o Victoria Falls (Zambia and Zimbabwe)
o Mount Kilimanjaro (Tanzania)
o Valley of the Kings (Egypt)

Pyramids at Giza

Valley of the Kings

Algeria

Lagos, Nigeria

N
W E
S

Seychelles

Victoria Falls

Mount Kilimanjaro

Glossary

ancient—from long ago

area—a specific place

continent—one of the seven main land areas on Earth; the continents are Africa, Antarctica, Asia, Australia, Europe, North America, and South America.

equator—an imaginary line around the center of Earth; the equator divides the planet into a northern half and a southern half.

hemispheres—halves of the globe; the equator and prime meridian divide Earth into different hemispheres.

landmark—an important structure or place

migrate—to travel from one place to another, often with the seasons

population—the number of people who live in an area

prime meridian—an imaginary line that runs vertically around Earth; the prime meridian divides the planet into a western half and an eastern half.

rain forest—a thick, green forest that receives a lot of rain

savannahs—grassslands with scattered trees

shrubs—short, woody plants

To Learn More

AT THE LIBRARY

Oxlade, Chris. *Introducing Africa*. Chicago, Ill.: Heinemann Library, 2014.

Riggs, Kate. *Zebras*. Mankato, Minn.: Creative Education, 2014.

Steele, Philip. *Ancient Egyptians*. New York, N.Y.: Kingfisher, 2012.

ON THE WEB

Learning more about Africa is as easy as 1, 2, 3.

1. Go to www.factsurfer.com.

2. Enter "Africa" into the search box.

3. Click the "Surf" button and you will see a list of related web sites.

With factsurfer.com, finding more information is just a click away.

Index

The images in this book are reproduced through the courtesy of: Eduard Kyslynskyy, front cover; sculpies, p. 4; Oleg Znamenskiy, p. 5; Guenter Guni, p. 8; Pichugin Dmitry, p. 9; PHOTOCREO Michal Bednarek, p. 10; Age Fotostock/ Superstock, p. 11; Thomas Marent/ Minden Pictures/ Corbis, p. 12 (top); blickwinkel/ Alamy, p. 12 (bottom); robertharding/ Superstock, p. 13 (top); shuttJD, p. 13 (bottom); Eric Isselee, p. 14 (left); Sergey Uryadnikov, p. 14 (top right); Audrey Snider-Bell, p. 14 (middle right); Mogens Trolle, p. 14 (bottom right); Francois Gagnon, p. 15; Nigel Pavitt/ JAI/ Corbis, p. 16; Peeter Viisimaa, p. 18; Bill Kret, p. 19; WitR, p. 21 (top left); Maxal Tamor, p. 21 (top right); Cristian Zamfir, p. 21 (bottom left); Przemyslaw Skibinski, p. 21 (bottom right).